D1396772

WHY·DO·BIRDS·

BUILD·NESTS?

Susan Horner

Illustrated by Nancy Munger

Moody Publishers

Chicago

ISBN: 0-8024-0922-9

1 3 5 7 9 10 8 6 4 2

Cover and internal design: Barbara Fisher / LeVan Fisher Design / barbfisher@earthlink.net
Internal design and production: Britt Menendez / bdesigns@sbcglobal.net

Printed in Italy

For my daughters
and all boys and girls everywhere in the world.
Each one of you is valuable, precious, and loved by God.

I give thanks for my husband and for each one of you (you know who you are) who prayed,
encouraged, or gave up your time to read and honestly share your thoughts.
You helped the idea become the books we now hold in our hands.

Special thanks to Michele Straubel and everyone at Moody Publishers
who had a part in this series.

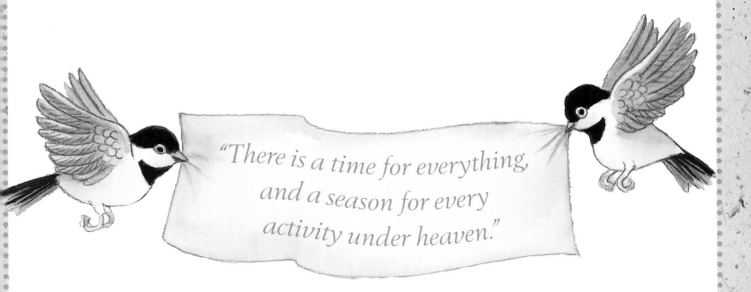

*"There is a time for everything,
and a season for every
activity under heaven."*

DEAR PARENTS,

Why Do Birds Build Nests? is the second book in the Miracle of Creation series. This gentle, modest series celebrates our Creator's wise design for reproduction.

Chickadees are an example of responsible sexuality. Their lives are ordered by the seasons. They cannot live contrary to the season they are in because they are ruled by instincts. But people were given the freedom to choose. As Ecclesiastes 3:11 says, "He has made everything beautiful in its time." When we ignore God's commands and timetable, we hurt both ourselves and our children.

This series was written to help you comfortably and gradually discuss biblical sexuality with your child. There are three books in the series: *Why Do Plants Grow?*, *Why Do Birds Build Nests?*, and *What Is God's Design for My Body?* At the back of the first two books are some fun family activities you may enjoy doing together.

Blessings,
Susan Horner

sn't it lovely to awaken to the singing of birds? Songbirds can sing up and down the musical scale because they have more muscles in their throats than other birds do. There are many different kinds of songbirds. Some sing flute-like trills, and others sing only a few loud notes. You can recognize the birds in the trees and fields near your home by listening for their special calls and songs.

A baby songbird learns its song by listening to its father and mother. When a male songbird sings, the females listen carefully to every single note. They can tell if he is grown-up enough to know his song, or if he is still practicing.

A meadowlark will not sing a love song to a robin, nor will a chickadee sing his song to a sparrow. God created birds to be attracted only to their own species.

God made every kind of bird. Then He said, "Have many young ones." And since the fifth day of creation until now, robins build cuplike nests for their beautiful blue eggs. Meadowlarks arrange dried grass roofs over their nests on the treeless prairies. Orioles weave hanging baskets for their babies to sway with the leaves, high in the trees.

Genesis 1:22 NCV

When warm breezes turn icy and daylight fades into long, dark nights, many birds fly away to warmer places. The chickadees stay. Eight to ten of them will band together. Each flock will have chickadees that hatched last spring, couples who just finished raising their first brood, and an older couple to lead them.

As golden autumn passes into gray winter, a young male and a young female will become best friends and pair off as a winter couple.

The couple will flit from branch to branch, calling back and forth to one another as they look for food. One hops along a branch, pecking at cones for seeds, while the other hangs upside down, pecking the underside of the branch to find sleeping bugs and insect eggs—the perfect breakfast for a pair of cheerful chickadees.

During the winter, nuthatches, brown creepers, and woodpeckers follow the chickadees because they are good lookouts for danger. The chickadees call to each other, "Chick-a-dee-dee, chick-a-dee-dee." A hawk flies over, and a sentry chickadee gives a warning "Zee-zee." All the birds stay very still until "Chick-a-dee-dee" rings through the woods again.

The lead chickadee gives a signal, and the flock takes to the sky. They bob up and down and glide. They land on goldenrod or ragweed poking through the snow. In an instant, they are off and flying again. They swoop down to land on clotheslines and trees in a human friend's backyard. A few bold chickadees fly to the hand offering them sunflower seeds. The shyer ones go to the feeders for sunflower seeds, blueberries, suet, and peanuts.

Tree holes are called cavities, and birds who use tree holes for nests are called cavity dwellers.

Young Mr. Chickadee waits for his turn at the feeder. He takes a seed with his beak and flies to a nearby tree. He cracks it open and nibbles away. He goes back for more. This time he carries the seed to his nighttime roosting tree. He tucks it into the ripply bark and saves it for later.

Chickadees usually sleep alone among the branches of pine and spruce trees or inside tree holes. But on extra cold nights, the flock huddles together inside a tree hole. They keep each other warm as icy winds and snow swirl outside their tree.

OVARY

EGG CELLS

NUCLEUS

CLOACA

After winter's longest night, each new day dawns earlier than the day before. Spring is on its way, even though trees still stand leafless and snow is on the ground. The longer hours of sunlight trigger chemical messengers inside the birds' bodies. These chemical messengers called **hormones** work like an alarm clock, ringing, "Wake up! Wake up!" And the young birds' bodies begin to develop in wonderful new ways.

Within the female's body is an **ovary**. It looks like a bunch of tiny grapes. Of course, they are not grapes at all. They are a cluster of egg cells. They do not look like the eggs you would find in a nest or at the grocery store. At this time they have no shell, no egg white, and no yellow yolk. Then what *do* the eggs have?

Each egg has a **nucleus**—a living speck—that holds all the information on how the female chickadee, and her parents, grandparents, and great-grandparents were made: their voices, type of beak, the colors in their feathers. Everything that makes her a cheerful chickadee is stored inside each tiny egg cell.

With longer hours of sunlight, the hormone alarm clock awakens the two **testes** inside the male chickadee's body. The testes grow larger as they make teeny-tiny **sperm** cells. A sperm is much smaller than an egg cell. Each microscopic sperm has a nucleus that holds a blueprint of how Mr. Chickadee and his parents, grandparents, and great-grandparents were made: their voices, type of beak, the colors in their feathers. All this information is stored inside each of his sperm.

The same hormones that caused the male and female birds' bodies to mature have also caused the winter couple to feel something more than friendship for each other.

Now the female chickadee twitters softly and flutters her wings as if to say, "Come and catch me!" Young Mr. Chickadee flies after her, and together they enjoy the wind beneath their wings.

Later, he boldly guards her as they flit from branch to branch. She encourages him by fluttering her wings and twittering like a baby bird. He hops over to her and offers his gift, a seed, which she accepts. Then he sings, "Fee-bee, fee-bee."

TESTES

SPERM CELL

CLOACA

The flying chases, gift giving, and singing continue. Whenever they are apart, they call to one another because a bond has formed between them that will last as long as they live. They have become Mr. and Mrs. Chickadee.

They leave the flock searching for a place to build a nest. After they claim a tree hole or a man-made nesting box, Mr. Chickadee guards the boundaries of their home. He chases away other male chickadees and loudly sings, "Fee-bee, fee-bee!" His song tells other chickadees, "Keep away. This is my home. You'll have to find another place."

Both birds clean the tree hole by carrying out wood chips and clutter. Then Mrs. Chickadee looks for dry grass, straw, and moss. With her beak full, she flies back to the tree.

For weeks she works at nest making from dawn to dusk, while Mr. Chickadee brings her food. Her pile gets higher and higher like a haystack. Then she shapes it into a soft bowl.

When the birds that flew away for the winter return, the chickadees are already flying with beaks full of straw, paper, and lost ribbons to tuck into their nests. With the return of these **migratory** birds, the spring air is filled with song. This is what King Solomon described more than 3,000 years ago as the time of the singing of the birds, the time when new life appears on the earth.

Song of Songs 2:12

Spring's warmth and light urges the trees' buds to open. On the leaves are caterpillars and grubs for Mrs. Chickadee to eat. This healthy insect diet helps the eggs inside her body to properly develop.

In the spring, furry animals and birds shed their winter coats, so Mrs. Chickadee finishes her nest with the soft fur and feathers she finds on the ground and bushes. The same hormones that caused her eggs to grow have also caused Mrs. Chickadee to lose her underbelly feathers. Her bare skin, called the **brood patch**, is sensitive to scratchy straw and grass, and the fur and feathers she uses to line her nest will feel soft and warm for both Mrs. Chickadee and her featherless babies.

Everything is ready. Mrs. Chickadee's brood patch is bare and warm. There are little soft caterpillars for baby food and a comfy nest that is being protected by Mr. Chickadee. Now is the perfect time for new baby birds.

But how does this happen?

Inside the mother bird's body an egg sitting on a yellow yolk moves from the ovary into the upper part of the egg tube. At the top of the egg tube, the egg waits to be **fertilized** with a sperm.

OVARY

SPERM AND EGG CELL

Fertilization of the egg takes place after the male and female have mated. First there was friendship, courtship, pair bonding, nest building, and now the mating time has come. As the Bible tells us, "There is a time for everything, and a season for every activity under heaven."

Mrs. Chickadee leaves the nest. She flies from branch to branch. Her mate flies after her. She softly sings while fluttering her wings and lifting her tail. Mr. Chickadee sings and flutters his wings. Then he hops onto Mrs. Chickadee's back. She raises her tail feathers so he can place his round body opening, called a **cloaca**, over her cloaca. Fluid carrying the father bird's sperm flows out from his body opening into her body.

Once the sperm have entered the mother bird's body, they swim up to the very top of her egg tube. One sperm will push into the egg cell. The nucleus of the egg and the nucleus of the sperm mix together, and the egg becomes fertilized.

An egg will wait at the top of the egg tube for several hours before moving down the tube to the next stop. If fertilization does not happen, a baby bird will not grow inside the egg. Most of the chicken eggs you buy at grocery stores are unfertilized eggs.

Ecclesiastes 3:1

The fertilized egg, sitting on its yellow yolk, moves down the tube and stops to be wrapped in egg white. Then the egg, having both yolk and white, moves farther down the tube to be wrapped in egg shell, which is made of **calcium carbonate** crystals.

Now the egg is ready to leave the mother bird's body. The pressing of the egg against the cloaca causes her to push. The cloaca stretches enough for the egg to slip through and land in the fluffy nest. The next day another egg moves from the mother's ovary into her egg tube. Each egg needs a sperm to fertilize it, so the male and female birds will mate again and again during this time of the "singing of the birds." This was God's plan when He said, "Have many young ones—let the birds grow in number on the earth."

After the nest is filled with six or seven white eggs with reddish brown spots, Mrs. Chickadee settles into the nest, covering them with her warm, bare skin. The eggs are so small that all seven can fit inside a tablespoon. The tiny new lives inside the fertilized eggs would not grow without their mother's warmth. Every few hours she stands up and turns the eggs, then sits back down. Mr. Chickadee brings her meals while she cares for their eggs.

Genesis 1:22 NCV

It is amazing and wonderful that, because of sperm and egg, a heart, two eyes, lungs, and the bones of a baby bird begin to form.

The growing life, or embryo, floats in its waterbed of egg white. The yellow yolk is food for the growing bird. Blood vessels spread around the yolk bring food into the baby bird's stomach. Some of the calcium from the shell will be absorbed to make strong bones. Air, carrying oxygen, passes through the egg shell for the baby bird.

After twelve or thirteen days under their mother's brood patch, one by one each tiny, featherless baby pecks a hole in its shell and pushes until the shell breaks open. The babies are blind and naked. Each has a bellybutton where the yolk was once connected to its stomach. A bright yellow line around each beak helps Mr. and Mrs. Chickadee see their babies' open mouths and quickly satisfy their cries for food.

Mr. and Mrs. Chickadee will fly back and forth from the nest to trees and sprouting plants, looking for caterpillars. Each day they must find at least 600 caterpillars to feed their babies.

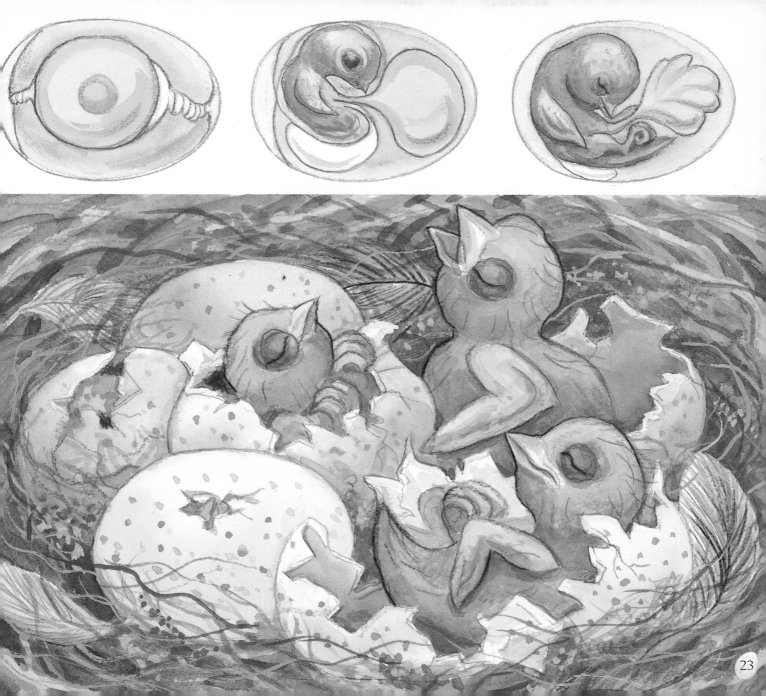

Around two weeks after they hatch, the feathered babies stretch and flutter their wings in the safety of their nest. In a few more days they stick out their heads and see the sky.

Their parents urge each one to flap its wings, step off the edge, and fly.

After they are out of the nest, the chickadee babies follow their parents, fluttering their wings, crying, "Dee-dee. Feed me." They open their mouths and wait for a parent to tuck food down their beaks. For the next two weeks Mr. and Mr. Chickadee will show their children how to feed themselves.

Our kind and loving Creator gave chickadees this **instinct** to care for their babies. Soon the young chickadees will be able to find their own food and water. When they are fully grown they will weigh as much as a quarter, dime, and nickel feel when you hold all three in your hand.

Once again, the seasons change. Summer drifts into autumn. Migrating birds fly off to warmer places. Mr. and Mrs. Chickadee join a small winter flock. Some of their children will come with them, and others will join another flock. Next spring when the air is filled with the singing of the songbirds, Mr. and Mrs. Chickadee will have more babies. Some of their older children will find mates, build nests, and together they will care for their babies. For "There is a time for everything, and a season for every activity under heaven."

Ecclesiastes 3:1

FUN • FAMILY • ACTIVITIES

1. Have fun watching birds—with binoculars if you have them.

2. Set up a birdbath. Birds enjoy taking baths and need to drink water every day. Be sure to clean and refill your birdbath with fresh water at least every other day. A bird scout will see it and tell other birds. Soon your birdbath will be a wildlife hangout.

3. Invite birds to a garden party by growing sunflowers, asters, bachelor buttons, zinnias, purple coneflower, and marigolds. When the flowers have finished blooming and are withered and dry, the birds will come and eat their seeds.

4. Open a bird restaurant. Once they find your feeder, they will keep coming back. Remember to hang your feeder at least five feet high or put it where a cat cannot catch the birds. Put decals on the window near your birdfeeder so that a bird will not hit the glass and break its neck.

5. Help birds build nests in the springtime. Mother birds will be looking for soft things to make comfy, warm nests for their coming babies. You can help by putting out short pieces of string and yarn. Be sure the string is only 3 to 4 inches long, or it could be dangerous for the birds. After you brush your dog or rabbit, stick the hair on fences or in trees for the birds to find and carry to their nests.

6. Set up a bird box for cavity dwelling birds. Be sure to place a protecting device over the entrance. This will make it more difficult for predators—squirrels, blue jays, and starlings—to reach into the nest and eat the eggs and babies. For nesting box dimensions and the size of the entrance hole, go to your local library or talk to an ornithologist (a scientist who works with birds) at your state park.

7. Look at some helpful web sites:

   www.fifthdaycreations.com

   www.wbu.com (wildbird unlimited)

   www.wildbirdcenter.com

Menu for your
Bird Restaurant

Just like you, birds have favorite foods:

Black oil sunflower seeds, served in any kind of feeder, for cardinals, purple finches, tufted titmice, chickadees, house finches, rosy finches, grosbeaks, nuthatches, chickadees, stellar jays, and scrub jays.

White Proso millet, served on the ground or high platforms, for red-winged blackbirds, mourning doves, towhees, juncos, and sparrows.

Thistle or Niger seeds, served from hanging tube feeders, for pine siskins, goldfinches, and purple finches.

Unsalted, broken peanuts for stellar jays, scrub jays, and chickadees.

For northern orioles, place an orange half onto an old stump or branch. You may want to hang a sugar water feeder near the orange. To prepare sugar water you will need four cups of water. Mix water with one cup of sugar. Do not use honey, because it quickly gets moldy and can make your visitors sick. Please do not use artificial sweeteners either.

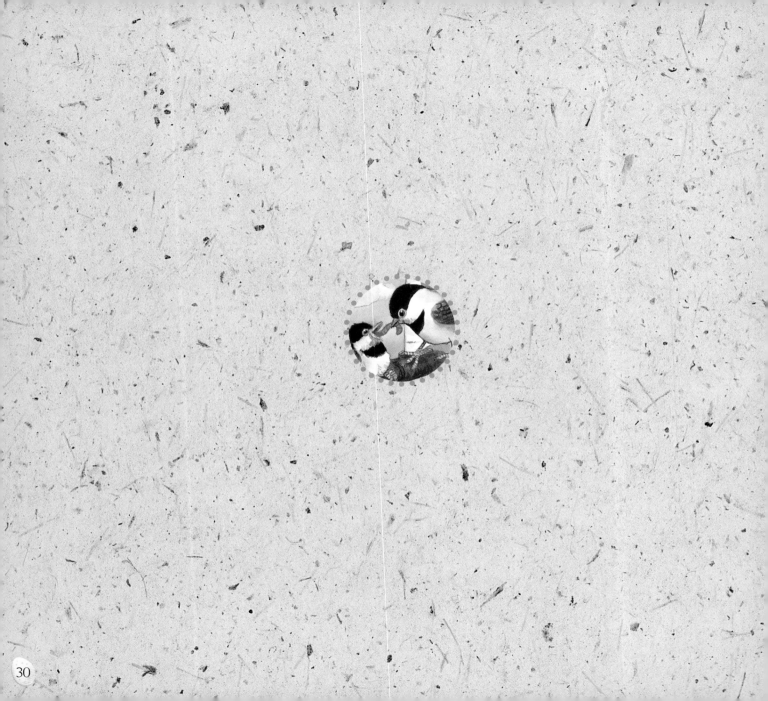

GLOSSARY

brood patch: Bare skin under a mother bird's belly that helps keep her eggs warm.

calcium carbonate: The material found in an egg shell that helps the baby bird form strong bones.

cavity dwellers: Birds who build nests in tree holes or other small spaces.

cloaca: The round opening in a male or female bird's body, under its tail.

embryo: The growing life that forms from a fertilized egg.

fertilized: An egg cell from the mother bird that has been joined with a sperm cell from the father bird.

hormones: Chemical messengers that cause changes in a bird's body.

instinct: Special knowledge given by God that helps birds and animals know how to mate, take care of their babies, and do other important things.

migratory: Birds that fly to warmer or cooler regions as the seasons change.

nucleus: A living speck inside a bird's egg or sperm cell that holds all of the information about that bird.

ovary: The organ in a female bird's body that produces tiny egg cells.

sperm: A tiny cell from the father bird that will enter one of the mother bird's egg cells to make a new baby bird.

testes: The two glands in a male bird's body that produce sperm cells.

SINCE 1894, Moody Publishers has been dedicated to equip and motivate people to advance the cause of Christ by publishing evangelical Christian literature and other media for all ages, around the world. Because we are a ministry of the Moody Bible Institute of Chicago, a portion of the proceeds from the sale of this book go to train the next generation of Christian leaders.

If we may serve you in any way in your spiritual journey toward understanding Christ and the Christian life, please contact us at www.moodypublishers.com.

"All Scripture is God-breathed and is useful for teaching, rebuking, correcting and training in righteousness, so that the man of God may be thoroughly equipped for every good work."
—2 TIMOTHY 3:16, 17

MOODY
PUBLISHERS
THE NAME YOU CAN TRUST®